Courageous Kids

CLAUDETTE COLVIN REFUSES TO MOVE

Courageous Kid of the Civil Rights Movement

by Ebony Joy Wilkins

illustrated by Mark Simmons

Consultant:
Tim Solie
Adjunct Professor of History
Minnesota State University, Mankato
Mankato, Minnesota

CAPSTONE PRESS
a capstone imprint

Graphic Library is published by Capstone Press, an imprint of Capstone.
1710 Roe Crest Drive, North Mankato, Minnesota 56003
www.capstonepub.com

Library of Congress Cataloging-in-Publication data
Names: Wilkins, Ebony, author.
Title: Claudette Colvin Refuses to Move : Courageous Kid of the Civil Rights Movement / by Ebony Joy Wilkins.
Other titles: Courageous kid of the civil rights movement
Description: North Mankato, MN : Capstone Press, [2020] | Series: Courageous kids | Includes bibliographical references and index. | Audience: Ages 8–11. | Audience: Grades 4–6. |
Summary: It's March 2, 1955, and an ordinary 15-year-old girl from Montgomery, Alabama is about to do something extraordinary. When a white bus driver orders Claudette Colvin to give up her seat for a white passenger, she refuses to move. After Claudette is arrested, her brave actions help inspire Civil Rights leaders to organize bus boycotts and perform similar acts to defy segregation laws. Eventually, Claudette's court case results in overturning Alabama's unconstitutional laws and provides greater freedom for black Americans everywhere—Provided by publisher.
Identifiers: LCCN 2020003288 (print) | LCCN 2020003289 (ebook) | ISBN 9781496685025 (hardcover) | ISBN 9781496688033 (paperback) | ISBN 9781496685063 (eBook PDF)
Subjects: LCSH: Colvin, Claudette, 1939– —Juvenile literature. | Montgomery Bus Boycott, Montgomery, Ala., 1955–1956—Juvenile literature. | African Americans—Civil rights—Alabama—Montgomery— Juvenile literature. | Montgomery (Ala.)—Social conditions—20th century—Juvenile literature. | African American teenage girls—Alabama—Montgomery—Biography—Juvenile literature. | African American teenagers—Alabama—Montgomery—Biography—Juvenile literature.
Classification: LCC F334.M753 W55 2020 (print) | LCC F334.M753 (ebook) | DDC 323.092 [B]—dc23
LC record available at https://lccn.loc.gov/2020003288
LC ebook record available at https://lccn.loc.gov/2020003289

EDITOR
Aaron J. Sautter

MEDIA RESEARCHER
Morgan Walters

ART DIRECTOR
Nathan Gassman

PRODUCTION SPECIALIST
Laura Manthe

DESIGNER
Ted Williams

Direct quotations appear in **bold italicized text** on the following pages:

Page 15: from *Claudette Colvin: Twice Toward Justice* by Phillip Hoose. New York: Melanie Kroupa Books, 2009.

Page 17: excerpt from interview with Claudette Colvin at the 2010 Library of Congress National Book Festival, https://www.youtube.com/watch?v=hMJi7RPSFig&feature=youtu.be.

Pages 19, 29 (top panel): from "Claudette Colvin: The 15-Year-Old Who Came Before Rosa Parks" by Taylor-Dior Rumble, BBC World Service, March 10, 2018, https://www.bbc.com/news/stories-43171799.

Page 29 (bottom panel): from "Claudette Colvin Honored by Montgomery Council," by Andrew J. Yawn, *Montgomery Advertiser*, February 21, 2017, https://www.montgomeryadvertiser.com/story/news/2017/02/21/claudette-colvin-honored-city-council-tonight/98197322/.

Printed and bound in the United states of America.
PA117

TABLE OF CONTENTS

After the U.S. Civil War (1861–1865) ended, several amendments were added to the U.S. Constitution. The 13th amendment officially ended slavery in the United States. The 14th amendment granted citizenship to black people. And the 15th amendment guaranteed male U.S. citizens the right to vote regardless of their race or color.

Black people were no longer enslaved in the United States. They were free to own land and live how they pleased.

However, during the late 1800s, many black people still faced terrible racism, persecution, and violence, especially in Southern states.

The Ku Klux Klan was a violent group of white supremacists. They often burned crosses in black people's yards to frighten them. They also beat and even killed black people. The Klan wanted to limit black people's rights and keep them from voting in elections.

During this time several Jim Crow laws were also passed in Southern states. These laws were named after a character created by white actor Thomas D. Rice. He covered his face with black makeup and made fun of black people on stage. From the 1870s to the 1950s, people in the South had to follow the Jim Crow laws. The laws forced black people to be segregated from white people.

Black people had to use separate restrooms.

They had to drink from their own water fountains.

Black people were often not allowed to eat in the same restaurants as white people.

WHITE ONLY

They had to sit in the balcony at movie theaters.

Black people even had to sit separately from white people on city buses.

By the 1950s, black people were sick and tired of being treated unfairly. But one teen girl was about to make a difference. Her brave actions would inspire black people to resist the unfair laws and start a major movement for change.

SICK AND TIRED

Claudette Colvin was born on September 5, 1939. She was adopted by Q.P. and Mary Anne Colvin soon after she was born.

Claudette grew up in a poor neighborhood in Montgomery, Alabama.

Life was difficult for black people in the South in the 1950s. It was hard for them to get a good education and a good job.

But Claudette's parents believed in her. They hoped she would one day help create a world where black people could achieve their dreams. They believed that if she worked hard in school she could make a difference.

Claudette was a curious person, and she loved to learn. In school she studied black spirituals, black history, and poems written by black authors.

Claudette enjoyed reading about Harriet Tubman. She loved how Tubman helped free hundreds of enslaved people in the 1850s.

Claudette also liked how Sojourner Truth, a formerly enslaved woman, helped fight for women's rights.

Claudette was inspired by these heroic black women and others like them. She wanted to make a difference like her heroes had.

It's not fair. We shouldn't be treated this way. We should be able to live the same way white people do.

Although Claudette didn't like the Jim Crow laws, there was little she could do about them. She had to follow the rules like everyone else.

Jim Crow laws also applied to the buses in Montgomery, Alabama. Black people had to sit in the back on the green and yellow city buses.

Even if the front seats were empty, black people had to stay in the back. There were no exceptions.

When the back seats were filled, black people had to stand instead. No matter how far they had to ride, they had to stay in the back half of the bus.

8

Breaking the bus rules was strictly forbidden. Claudette remembered hearing about two black men who were traveling from up North.

They had decided to ride a city bus and sat in one of the front rows behind the bus driver.

You boys need to move to the back.

The men ignored the driver's demand. They had paid their fare and didn't think they'd done anything wrong.

The police arrested them for breaking the law and later sent them home. Claudette thought a lot about what the men had done.

Breaking the rules meant breaking the law. And that usually meant big trouble for black people, like beatings or going to jail.

Claudette wasn't a troublemaker. She knew the rules and followed them. But that didn't mean she had to like them.

PAID FARE

On March 2, 1955, Claudette and her friends got out of school early.

The group hurried toward the city bus stop on Dexter Avenue.

The bus stop was across the street from Dexter Avenue Baptist Church. Dr. Martin Luther King Jr. served as the church's pastor.

Dr. King was a leader of the Civil Rights Movement. Dr. King believed that all people should have equal rights and be treated with respect.

Look, there's Dr. King. I've heard him speak before.

Me too. He's fighting for all of us to have equal rights.

Here comes the bus.

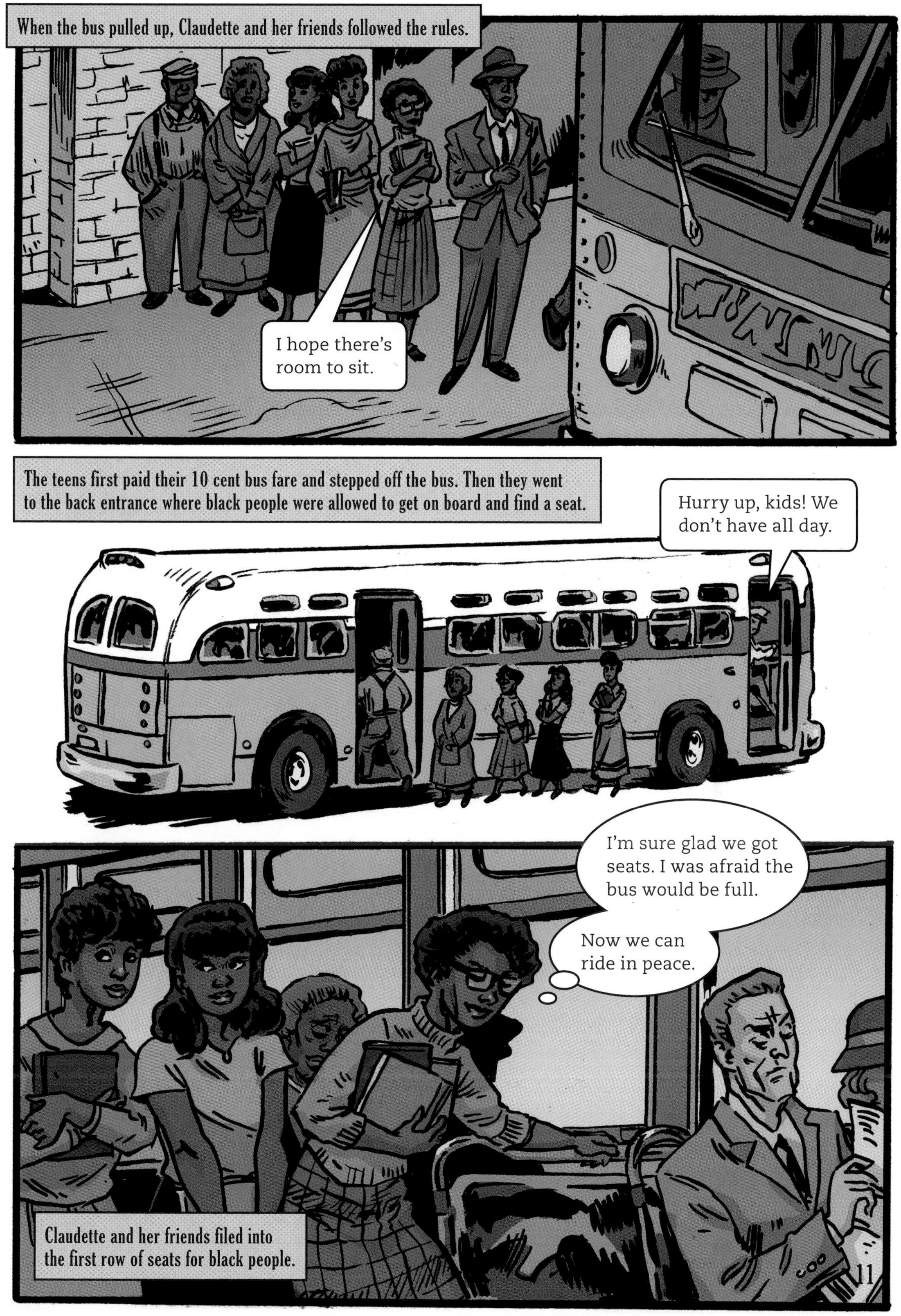
When the bus pulled up, Claudette and her friends followed the rules.
I hope there's room to sit.
The teens first paid their 10 cent bus fare and stepped off the bus. Then they went to the back entrance where black people were allowed to get on board and find a seat.
Hurry up, kids! We don't have all day.
I'm sure glad we got seats. I was afraid the bus would be full.
Now we can ride in peace.
Claudette and her friends filed into the first row of seats for black people.

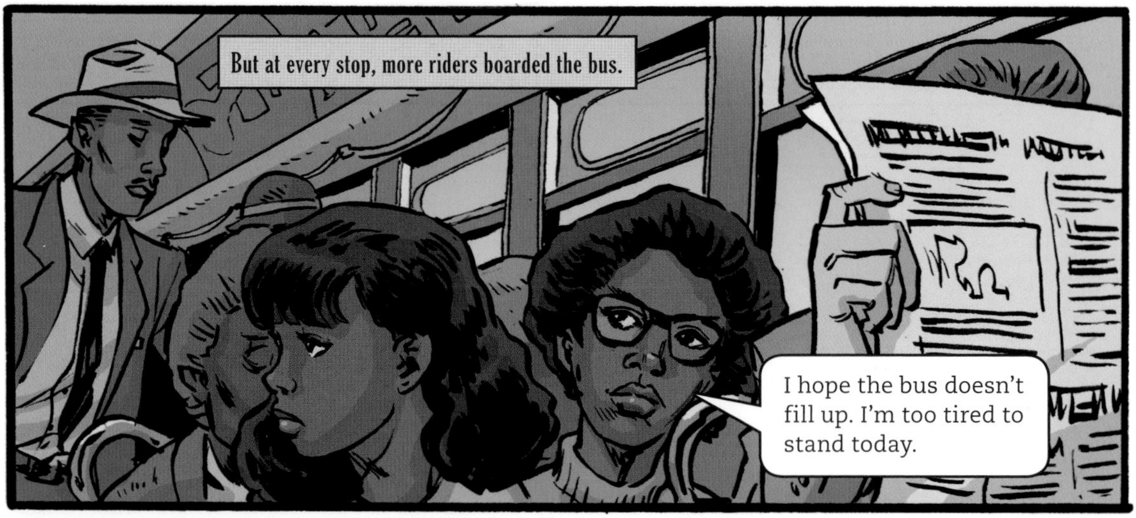
But at every stop, more riders boarded the bus.
I hope the bus doesn't fill up. I'm too tired to stand today.

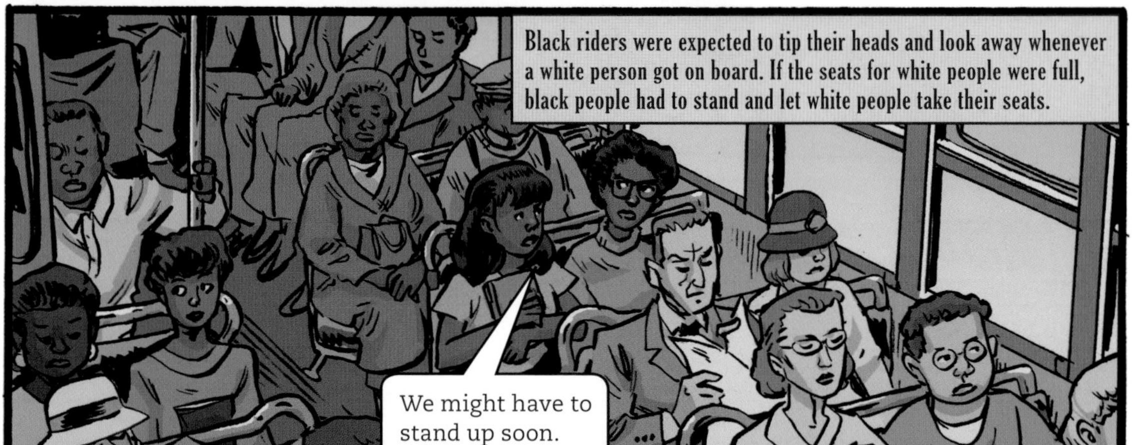
Black riders were expected to tip their heads and look away whenever a white person got on board. If the seats for white people were full, black people had to stand and let white people take their seats.
We might have to stand up soon.
Some days black riders got to sit. Other days they had to stand. Claudette had a bad feeling about this day.

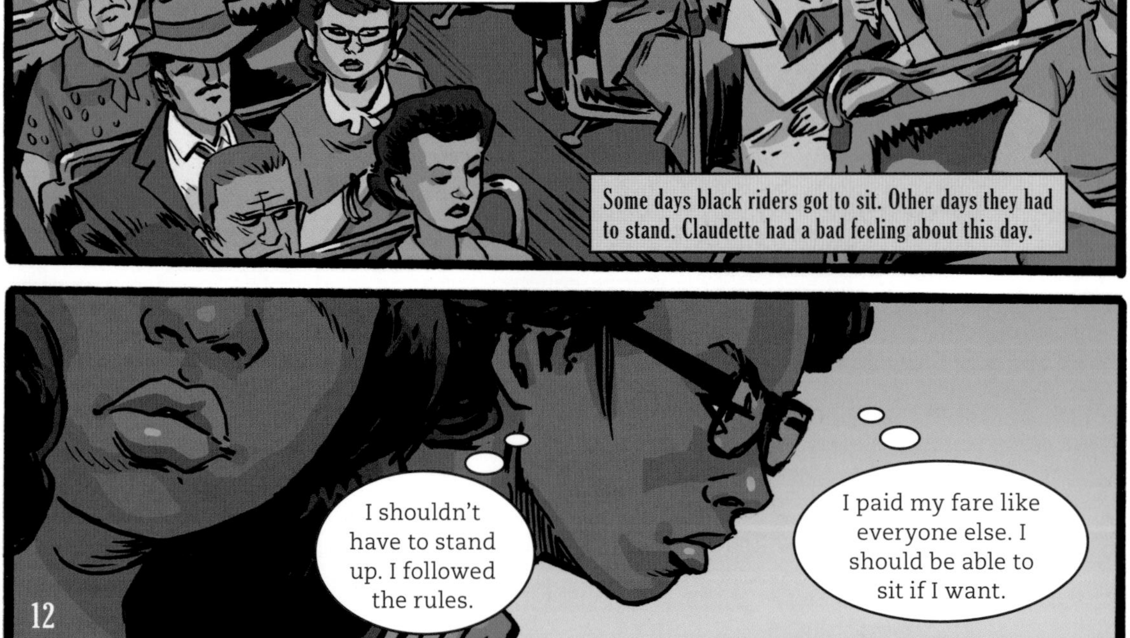
I shouldn't have to stand up. I followed the rules.
I paid my fare like everyone else. I should be able to sit if I want.

At the next stop, a white woman got on board. But the white section was full. The black section was full too. There were no empty seats left.

I'm *not* getting up!

Move it, girls! I need the front row.

The bus driver, Robert W. Cleere, yelled for Claudette and her friends to get out of their seats. The rules said that all the black people in a row had to move. Claudette's friends got up and moved, but she ignored the driver's demands.

Claudette thought about Harriet Tubman and Sojourner Truth. She thought about Dr. King. What would they do in her place?

Claudette, *get up. Don't cause any trouble.*

13

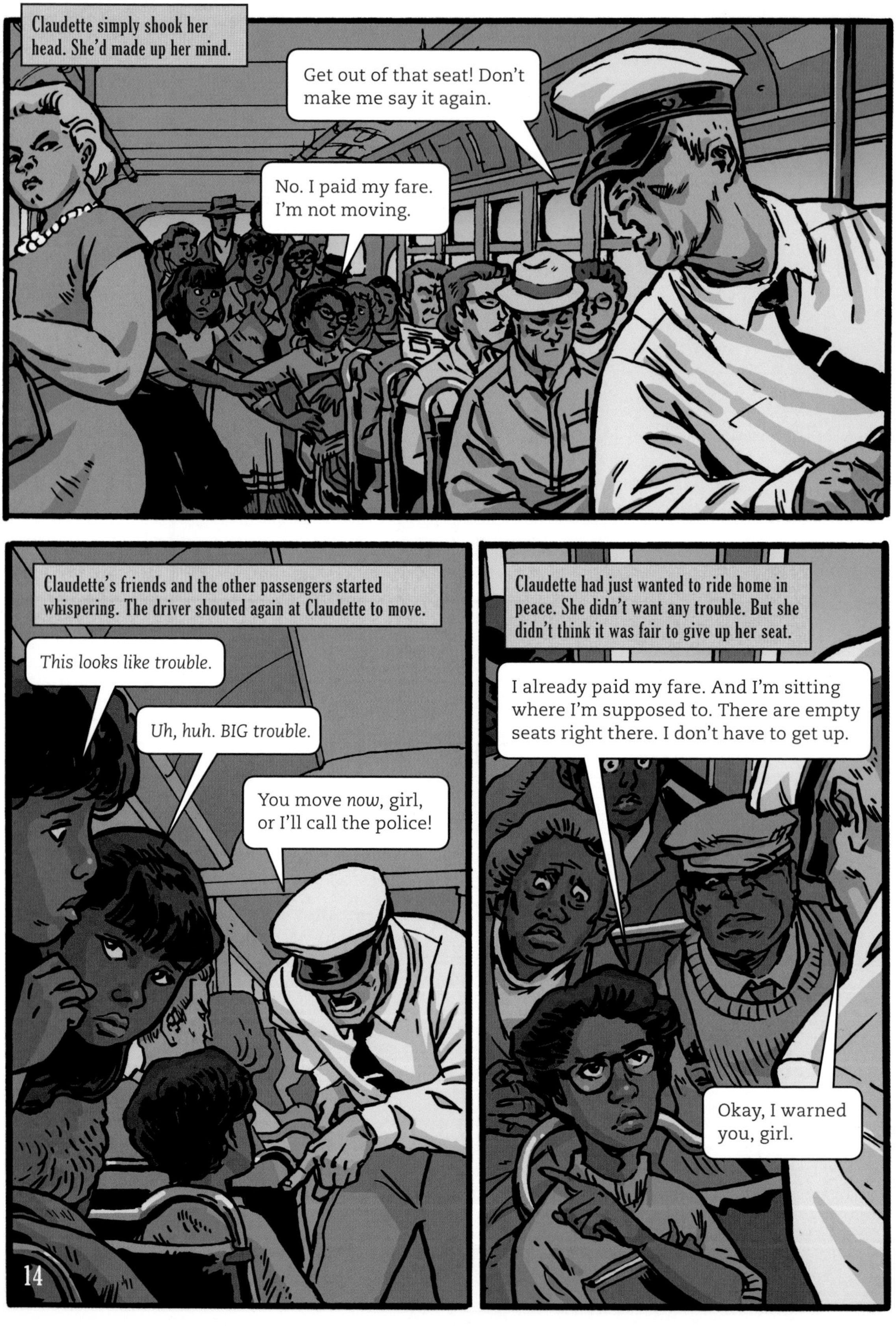
Claudette simply shook her head. She'd made up her mind.
Get out of that seat! Don't make me say it again.
No. I paid my fare. I'm not moving.
Claudette's friends and the other passengers started whispering. The driver shouted again at Claudette to move.
This looks like trouble.
Uh, huh. BIG trouble.
You move *now*, girl, or I'll call the police!
Claudette had just wanted to ride home in peace. She didn't want any trouble. But she didn't think it was fair to give up her seat.
I already paid my fare. And I'm sitting where I'm supposed to. There are empty seats right there. I don't have to get up.
Okay, I warned you, girl.

The driver pulled the bus to the next corner where a police car was waiting.

Hey, officers! I've got a troublemaker on board!

This is your last chance to move, girl.

But Claudette didn't move. She had paid her fare like everyone else and deserved to stay in her seat.

Several years later, Claudette recalled, "I was tired of hoping for justice. When my moment came, I was ready."

No. I didn't do anything wrong. I'm not moving.

ARRESTED!

You move out of that seat like you were told, girl!

No, sir. I paid my fare. It's my constitutional right.

One officer grabbed Claudette's arm and pulled her out of her seat. Her books scattered around the floor of the bus.

The officer dragged Claudette like a rag doll to the bus's back door.

Let me go! I paid my fare!

The police officers put Claudette in the back of their car and handcuffed her like a criminal.

Claudette watched as the bus rolled by without her.

You should have done as you were told, kid. Now you'll have to come with us.

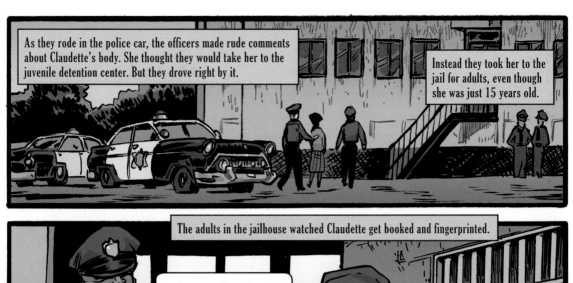

As they rode in the police car, the officers made rude comments about Claudette's body. She thought they would take her to the juvenile detention center. But they drove right by it.

Instead they took her to the jail for adults, even though she was just 15 years old.

The adults in the jailhouse watched Claudette get booked and fingerprinted.

Why am I here? I did nothing wrong.

You're in trouble now!

Quiet!

Why didn't you get up when the driver told you to, girl?

But Claudette didn't answer. She knew she hadn't done anything wrong. But no one was listening to her.

Years later Claudette recalled thinking, "*History had me glued to the seats ... It felt like Harriet Tubman was pushing me down on one shoulder and Sojourner Truth was pushing me down on the other.*"

"Let me out of here!"

"I want to go home!"

"I didn't do it!"

The officer slammed the cell door closed, locking Claudette inside. She could hear other people yelling in the cells nearby.

Claudette was terrified. She didn't know what was happening, or what would happen to her in that small cell.

"Dear Lord, help me survive."

Claudette had heard about black people being beaten in jail. Some were even killed when no one was looking. But she wasn't ready to die.

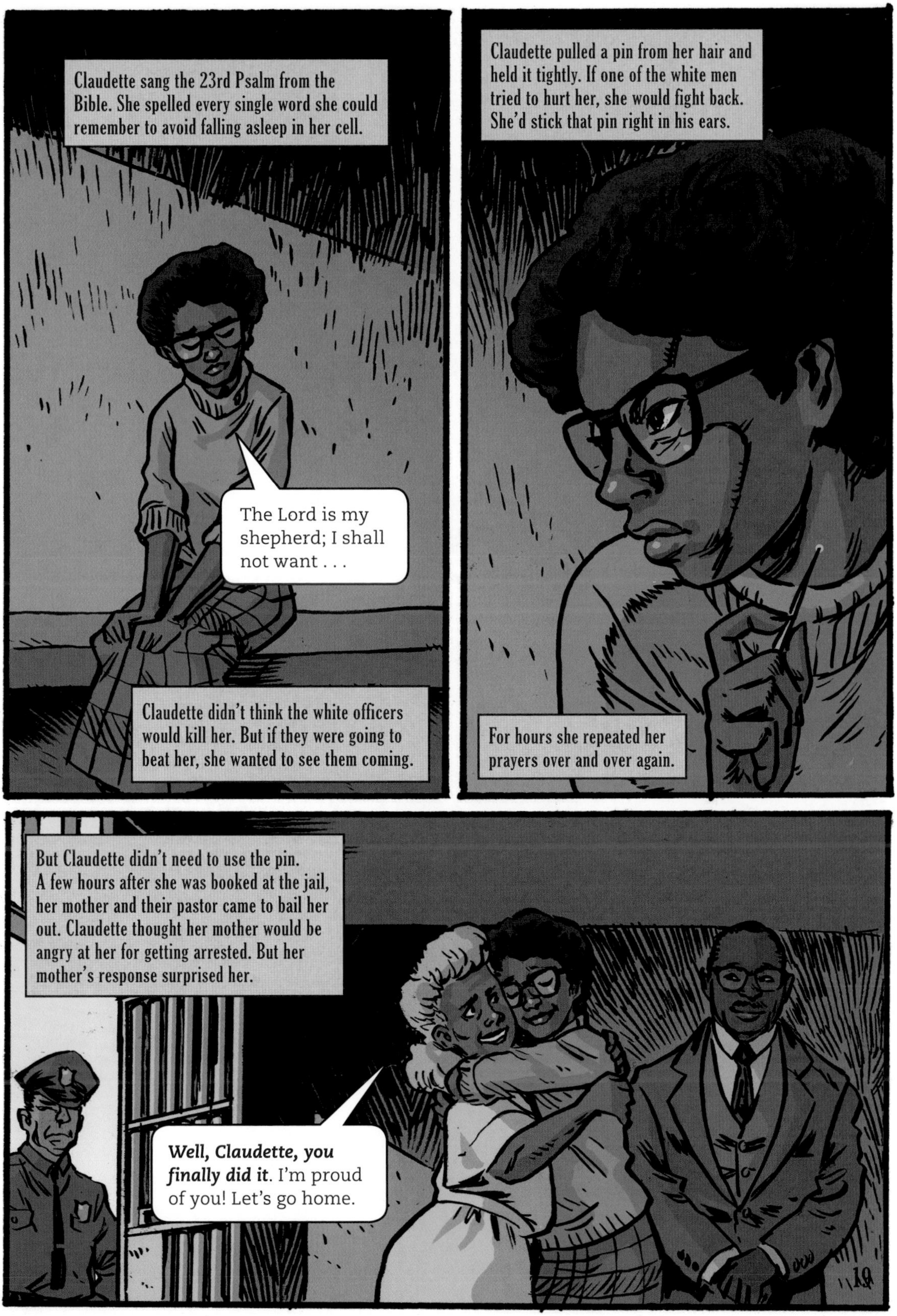
Claudette sang the 23rd Psalm from the Bible. She spelled every single word she could remember to avoid falling asleep in her cell.
The Lord is my shepherd; I shall not want . . .
Claudette didn't think the white officers would kill her. But if they were going to beat her, she wanted to see them coming.
Claudette pulled a pin from her hair and held it tightly. If one of the white men tried to hurt her, she would fight back. She'd stick that pin right in his ears.
For hours she repeated her prayers over and over again.
But Claudette didn't need to use the pin. A few hours after she was booked at the jail, her mother and their pastor came to bail her out. Claudette thought her mother would be angry at her for getting arrested. But her mother's response surprised her.
Well, Claudette, you finally did it. I'm proud of you! Let's go home.

Although Claudette's parents were proud of her, they knew that white people might be angry about what she'd done. Her family stayed up that whole night to keep watch in case any white men came knocking.

Go keep watch at the back door. I'll watch the front.

There's no way I'm letting anyone hurt my little girl or family tonight.

Claudette's father sat by the window with his shotgun ready. Some friends and neighbors helped keep watch too.

The Colvin family made it through the night unharmed. But news of her arrest quickly made it into the newspaper.

t On Indefinite Probation

Negro Girl Found Guilty Of Segregation Violation

Now everyone will know what happened.

That's right, Claudette. You'll have to be extra careful now.

For the next few days, Claudette feared that someone might try to hurt her or her family. Before going to bed, she made sure no one was hiding outside.

No one is out there, honey. Go to sleep.

When she walked down the street, she watched to make sure no white people followed her.

At school, Claudette's friends and classmates all wanted to talk about the day she got arrested and dragged off the bus.

Did you see any bad guys?

What was jail like?

It was pretty scary. I didn't know what was going to happen. But I know I didn't do anything wrong.

FIGHTING FOR JUSTICE

A few weeks after Claudette's arrest, Dr. Martin Luther King Jr. gathered members of the black community at Dexter Avenue Baptist Church. They talked about the unfair Jim Crow laws and how they could fight them.

We cannot, we will not, let the treatment of this poor girl stand.

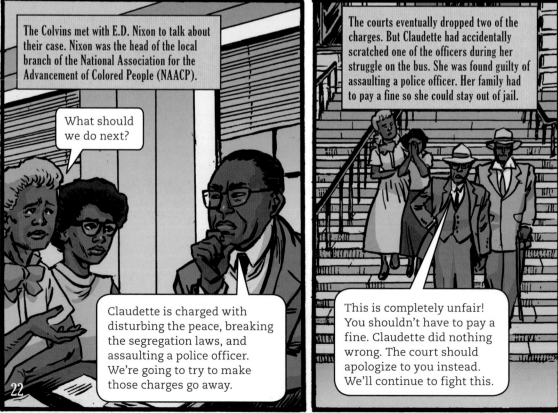

The Colvins met with E.D. Nixon to talk about their case. Nixon was the head of the local branch of the National Association for the Advancement of Colored People (NAACP).

What should we do next?

Claudette is charged with disturbing the peace, breaking the segregation laws, and assaulting a police officer. We're going to try to make those charges go away.

The courts eventually dropped two of the charges. But Claudette had accidentally scratched one of the officers during her struggle on the bus. She was found guilty of assaulting a police officer. Her family had to pay a fine so she could stay out of jail.

This is completely unfair! You shouldn't have to pay a fine. Claudette did nothing wrong. The court should apologize to you instead. We'll continue to fight this.

Dr. Martin Luther King Jr. worked with other community leaders to raise money for Claudette's legal costs. He also spoke out about fighting the unfair Jim Crow laws.

The laws are unjust! It is time to change them. It is time for us to act!

That's right!

Amen!

Change the laws!

Mrs. Rosa Parks knew Claudette and her family. She was the leader for Claudette's church youth group. She was also secretary of the local NAACP branch and a civil rights activist.

Some folks think you're just a rebellious teenager.

But I know you're mature and know about your rights.

Yes, ma'am. I guess that day my head was full of black history and all the pain and torment we've suffered.

Look at all of these people! I was just tired of Jim Crow.

We're tired of it too. We all want to help you.

Claudette had decided on the bus that day that she wasn't going to be treated unfairly anymore. She didn't know her actions would spark a movement. But soon Civil Rights leaders from all over the south began arriving to take a stand against Jim Crow laws.

23

On December 1, 1955, Rosa Parks refused to give up her seat on a bus.

I need these seats. You need to move.

I don't think I should have to stand up.

Then I'm calling the police.

Rosa Parks was arrested and taken to jail, just like Claudette had been several months before.

That night, Civil Rights leaders worked together to arrange a boycott of Montgomery's buses. They wanted to force white people to pay attention to the unjust laws.

These flyers should help get the word out and help our cause.

This boycott will surely help bring great change for our city.

A few days later, on December 5, the Montgomery Bus Boycott started. Ninety percent of black folks refused to get on the city buses in Montgomery.

During the boycott, black people carpooled, took taxis, or walked for miles in bad weather.

After a while, the boycott started having an effect. The city was losing money. Sometimes white police officers stopped carpool drivers to try to break the boycott.

You've got too many people in your car. You'll have to pay a fine for that.

However, many white people in Montgomery had no plans to get rid of segregation or Jim Crow laws. They were ready to do whatever it took to stop the boycott.

On January 30, 1956, white men firebombed Martin Luther King Jr.'s home.

He and his family survived, but their home was destroyed.

Another bombing happened at E.D. Nixon's home two days later.

But the violent acts did not discourage the boycotters. Black people stayed off the buses and kept walking. The seats in the back of the buses stayed empty for more than a year.

25

While the boycott was happening, Civil Rights leaders and attorney Fred Gray decided to fight the bus segregation law in court. Gray filed the case, known as *Browder v. Gayle*, at the local U.S. District Court.

Thank you for working on this case, Fred. We need your help.

It's my honor. We'll keep fighting for justice and to change the laws.

News spread fast about the court case. Claudette was asked to testify during the trial about the unfair Jim Crow laws. The court case also included Aurelia S. Browder, Susie McDonald, and Mary Louise Smith. The women all had stories to tell. Jeanetta Reese was also going to testify, but she dropped out after being threatened by white people.

Tell us what happened that day, miss.

I paid my fare that day, and I sat in the right section. There were other open seats there. I tried to tell them, but no one would listen. The policeman dragged me off of the bus and took me to jail.

On June 5, 1956, the judges in Montgomery, Alabama, determined that bus segregation was unconstitutional.

But local officials were angry and appealed the court's decision. So the *Browder v. Gayle* case went to the U.S. Supreme Court.

Several months later the Supreme Court ruled to end bus segregation for good. The ruling put an end to the unfair bus laws and the bus boycott. Claudette, and black people everywhere, had won.

We're so proud of you!

You did it, baby girl!

Your actions have helped spark a movement that will change the world.

It's so nice to sit up front!

After the law changed, Claudette enjoyed the freedom to sit anywhere she liked on a bus. She could even sit directly behind the driver!

Claudette was thrilled about the changes in the law. People, both white and black, could sit wherever they liked on the city buses.

But many white people were still angry about the changes. They lashed out at black people and sometimes attacked them. Claudette no longer felt safe staying in Montgomery. At age 18, she boarded a bus for New York to start a new life.

Claudette moved to the Bronx in New York City. There she took a job as a nurse's aide to support her growing family.

Claudette lived a quiet life in New York. She never talked about being arrested or changing any laws.

When asked later about why she didn't say anything, she said, *"New York is a completely different culture to Montgomery, Alabama. Most of the people didn't have a problem with us sitting on the bus . . . I didn't want to discuss it with them."*

The day Claudette refused to give up her seat will now forever be honored in Montgomery, Alabama. In 2017 the Montgomery City Council named March 2 as Claudette Colvin Day.

Mayor Todd Strange proclaimed, *"She was an early foot soldier in our civil rights, and we did not want this opportunity to go by without declaring March 2 as Claudette Colvin Day to thank her for her leadership in the modern day Civil Rights Movement."*

29

GLOSSARY

activist (AK-tih-vist)—a person who works for social or political change

amendment (uh-MEND-muhnt)—a change made to a law or legal document

appeal (uh-PEEL)—to ask another court to review a case already decided by a lower court

boycott (BOY-kot)—an organized act in which a group of people refuse to buy or use a product or service to make a protest

civil rights (SI-vil RYTS)—the rights that all people have to freedom and equal treatment under the law

Jim Crow laws (JIM KROH LAWZ)—unfair laws that once forced black Americans to live separately from white people, especially in the South

NAACP—the National Association for the Advancement of Colored People, a civil rights organization that works to protect the freedoms of African American people

racism (RAY-siz-uhm)—the belief that one race is better than another race

segregation (seg-ruh-GAY-shuhn)—the practice of keeping groups of people apart, especially based on race

white supremacist (WITE soo-PREM-uh-sist)—a person who believes that the white race is superior to all other races

READ MORE

Llanas, Sheila. *Children in the Civil Rights Era*. Lake Elmo, MN: Focus Readers, 2019.

London, Martha. *Claudette Colvin*. Minneapolis: Discover Roo, an imprint of Pop!, 2020.

Small, Cathleen. *Claudette Colvin: Civil Rights Activist*. New York: Cavendish Square, 2020.

INTERNET SITES

Claudette Colvin
https://kids.britannica.com/kids/article/Claudette-Colvin/544733

Claudette Colvin Biography
https://www.biography.com/activist/claudette-colvin

Claudette Colvin : The 15-Year-Old Who Came Before Rosa Parks
https://www.bbc.com/news/stories-43171799

INDEX